AFTER THE WAR
WAS OVER

AFTER THE

168 masterpieces by

WAR WAS OVER

Magnum photographers

Werner Bischof   René Burri   Cornell Capa
Robert Capa   Henri Cartier-Bresson
Bruce Davidson   Elliott Erwitt   Burt Glinn
Ernst Haas   Philippe Halsman   Erich Lessing
Inge Morath   Marc Riboud   David Seymour
Marilyn Silverstone   Dennis Stock   Kryn Taconis

Introduction by Mary Blume

Harcourt Brace Jovanovich, Publishers
San Diego   New York   London

First published in the United States of America
by Harcourt Brace Jovanovich, Inc.

© 1985 by Thames and Hudson Ltd, London

Requests for permission to make copies of any
part of the work should be mailed to:
Permissions, Harcourt Brace Jovanovich, Publishers,
Orlando, Florida 32887

LIBRARY OF CONGRESS CATALOGING IN PUBLICATION DATA
Main entry under title:

After the war was over.

   "168 masterpieces by Magnum photographers."
   1. Europe — History — 1945-   — Pictorial works. 2. Europe —
Social life and customs — 1945-   — Pictorial works. 3. Europe —
Social conditions — 20th century — Pictorial works.
I. Bischof, Werner Adalbert, 1916-1954.
D1058.A63   1985   940.55   85-809
ISBN 0-15-103960-7

Printed and bound in Japan

First American Edition
A B C D

AFTER THE WAR WAS OVER

First the celebrations: the bonfires, bunting, conga lines, churchbells, the feeling of thanksgiving and release. In Britain on VE Day there was a violent early morning thunderstorm, just as in the last hours of peace in September 1939, but the day was perfect, warm and sunny, and it lasted until 10:30 p.m. because the country was still on double summer time. In London dogs wore huge tricolored ribbons and three women, including a duchess, kissed the socialite "Chips" Channon when he stopped by the Ritz before luncheon. "We went out eight times altogether and were given a great reception," the King wrote in his diary.

That night, for the first time in nearly six years, London was floodlighted, its wounds hidden under a great skyline dominated by the gold cross of St Paul's. And for the first time since 1939 Britons heard a weather forecast: "sporadic rain over the whole country." Winston Churchill, who would be voted out of office within weeks, appeared amid cheers — "That's 'im, that's 'is little old lovely bald 'ead," Mollie Panter-Downes heard a cockney cry — and he urged his countrymen not to forget the effort still needed to defeat Japan. Perhaps because three months of the Japanese war lay ahead or perhaps because of the sudden shock of peace, the writer John Lehmann felt that people were more dazed than excited, "like cripples taking their first steps after a miracle healing."

In Holland flags flew from windmills and RAF crews bringing in food were pelted with tulips. Oslo was still in enemy hands on VE Day because the German general in command had no one to surrender to. He finally capitulated to four surprised war correspondents, three airforce officers and two press photographers. Spain, Portugal, Sweden and Switzerland won no applause for breaking off relations with Germany upon its defeat, and on the day of defeat Heinrich Himmler shaved off his mustache and prepared to flee. He was caught but when identified on 24 May, he bit on a cyanide capsule and escaped the gallows at Nuremberg that claimed ten of his Nazi colleagues.

In Rome, said a correspondent, the news of VE Day was "taken with the helpless and tired shrug of the defeated." Parisians, whose hearts had burst at their own liberation the previous summer, left the wilder celebrating to the very young. And even the very young sometimes were worn out. Audie Murphy, the most decorated soldier in the US Army and not yet old enough to vote at the war's end, heard the shouts of victory at Lyons and suddenly was weary. "I could feel the blood drain out. My blood pressure went way down and stayed there and I've been tired ever since," he said many years later. On 9 May, after four days of street fighting, 90,000 German troops surrendered to Patton's Third Army west of Prague, while the first Russian tanks entered from the East.

The term VE Day had been coined by the US Office of War Mobilization. In time people would wonder if, after the war was over, it really was over. VE Day itself began with a sort of premonitory confusion for it was celebrated on 8 May in the West and on 9 May in the East, when a second surrender ceremony was held in Berlin at the Russians' insistence. The first ceremony, in a boys' school at Reims, was over very quickly; the

5

second began an hour late because the Russians were on Central European time and it ended with a four-hour meal, at the close of which even the interpreters could not understand the toasts.

To a discerning ear, the word "peace" had a slightly hollow ring. "Long before the war ended in May of 1945, it was clear there would be no peace," Theodore H. White wrote in 1954. Duff Cooper, hearing the last "All Clear" and the peal of victory bells in Paris, felt his eyes fill with tears. "The Duke of Wellington was right," he thought, "when he said a victory is the greatest tragedy in the world except a defeat."

The flatness of Harry Truman's prose makes the facts nearly bearable: "More people faced starvation and even death for want of food during the year following the war than during all the war years combined," he wrote.

Landscapes were flattened, buildings broken, farmland smashed by battle. It seemed as if nothing would ever grow again, as if there were only two seasons, cold and colder. "Though April has come with palms and lilacs/ I hear nothing now, as though it had snowed all night," the Greek poet George Seferis wrote in the spring of 1946.

A strip of gaily-striped wallpaper beside a gutted building, a sculpted *putto* dancing in the ruins of Warsaw, plumes of smoke in leaden skies. It was strangely empty and quiet and it stank. "It smelled of dust, oil, gunpowder and greasy metal; of drains and vermin; of sweat and vomit, dirty socks and excrement; of decay and burning and the unburied dead," wrote the British journalist Richard Mayne.

In Holland, adults subsisted on the caloric requirements of a six-year-old child. The worst was Eastern Europe. "I was ready to declare — I admit it openly — that a curse hangs over this part of Europe and nothing can be done about it," the Polish poet Czeslaw Milosz wrote. "Had I been given the chance, perhaps I would have blown the country to bits, so that mothers would no longer cry over their seventeen-year-old sons and daughters who died on the barricades, so that the grass would no longer grow over the ashes of Treblinka and Maidenek and Auschwitz, so that the notes of a harmonica player under a gnarled pine would no longer float over the nightmarish pits and dunes on the city outskirts. Because there is a kind of pity that is unbearable. And so one blows it up, at least in one's mind; that is, one is possessed by a single desire: not to look."

Germans did not use the word "defeat." 1945 was *Zusammenbruch* (total collapse) or *Jahr Null* (Year Zero). More than half the German men who would have been twenty-one in 1945 were missing, maimed or killed. Seven million European houses had been destroyed or badly damaged, five million of them German. Children ran after railroad trains screaming for food. On 30 January 1946, the bürgermeister of Stuttgart reported that the city had available 60,000 pairs of shoes, 71 overcoats and 220 suits for a population of 330,000. The same year, Germans began picking bricks out of the rubble and cleaning them off by hand. They reprocessed a total of 1.7 billion bricks that way. W. H. Auden, who had been sent to Germany with the Morale Division of the US Strategic Bombing Survey, wrote from Darmstadt: "The town outside which we live was ninety-two percent destroyed in thirty minutes. You can't imagine what it looks like unless you see it with your own eyes. We are billetted in the house of a Nazi who committed suicide and also poisoned his wife, children and grandchildren. The work is interesting but I'm near crying sometimes."

Germany was divided nominally into four zones and actually into two, East and West. The Germans were docile — "just as good at being defeated as they had been at waging war," a soldier in the British army sardonically noted; he was Dutch-born and had lived through the frightful German occupation of his country. In the British zone on 12 June 1945, Field Marshal Montgomery authorized troops to talk and play with German children. The Americans, whose homeland had not been under attack, gave out smiles and K rations, after a brief nonfraternization policy. The French, the only occupying force to have been defeated by the Germans, were determined to look smart and act confident. General de Lattre de Tassigny instructed his army to be wary of German women and to remember, if ever they felt inferior because of losing their war, that France had on several occasions occupied Germany, starting in the epoch of Louis XIV.

There were more buildings standing in Vienna than in the German cities, but the Russian occupants reduced food rations. "After seven years of war, I thought this was the way one lived," said Ernst Haas, who was born in Vienna. He felt the need to photograph the life around him: "It was so human, it seemed to call for graphic expression." One day, on a fashion assignment with Inge Morath, who was then a magazine writer and editor, he saw a group of women waiting at the East Station to see if their sons or husbands would be on one of the trains that arrived sporadically, and without warning, from the Eastern zones. He dropped Morath and the model and photographed the women holding out pictures of their men to the haggard revenants. The men in the pictures usually had happy, plump prewar faces and few of them came back.

"I wanted to show the woman as the real unknown soldier," Haas says. "She suffers the most in wars and no one writes about her or gives her veteran's benefits. She is just in the background during everything." No, he says, he never spoke to the waiting women: "If you speak, you get involved."

In Naples, urchins robbed American supply trucks and pockets with wondrous agility. In Rome, Edmund Wilson, touring Europe for The New Yorker and eating in an outdoor restaurant with his back to the railing, did not at first notice the crowd grabbing food from diners' plates. "The management sent out bouncers who dispersed the mob, knocking one old woman down with a blow to the head." Mussolini's pride, the Cinecittà film studio, had become a refugee camp and Roberto Rossellini and Vittorio De Sica were obliged to shoot in the streets. Their beautiful and shattering films were later given a comfortable label, "neo-realism."

Unlike Rome, Milan had taken heavy bombing and looked, someone said, like a slice of hell. Milan began to rebuild within a few weeks of the war's end and Toscanini was invited to return from America to conduct the re-opening of La Scala. On 11 May 1948, the

7

eighty-one-year-old Maestro raised his baton and loud-speakers carried the music to tens of thousands waiting outside.

The worst was over. Throughout Europe there was a will to start life anew, a great surge of idealism, a rush to give practical aid. There were organizations such as UNRRA (United Nations Relief and Rehabilitation Administration) doing dogged and spectacular work, and there were individuals such as the Swiss woman who went to Italy in 1945 to start a school for orphans in Rimini. "We felt there was no end to the possibilities, we felt that everything we did was important and that we could do it," she says. "I feel sorry for my children today who cannot even understand such a spirit and who see nothing but limits and ends."

Europe was bankrupt: it was a time for organizing and counting. Sometimes accounting replaced accountability. The Germans reckoned the *per diem* reparation due a prisoner in a concentration camp at five marks, minimum, and in August 1945, when the Allies were deciding on the indictment for the Nuremberg trials, the French insisted that every bottle of champagne the enemy had pinched be listed.

It was a way of dealing with the immeasurable. It is easier to enumerate than to describe six million dead in the Holocaust or the thirty million refugees who in 1945 were straggling across Europe. It was the greatest migration in human history. New bureaucratic labels were invented: Displaced Persons, Post-Hostility Refugees, Non-Repatriatees, Infiltrees, Uncovered Children. Germany took in *Volksdeutsche* (ethnic German) refugees at a rate that sometimes rose to 40,000 a week,

an act of charity that was to provide manpower for the German recovery.

Germany had to recover. The German philosopher Theodor Adorno had said in despair, "To write poetry after Auschwitz is barbaric," but the former French premier Léon Blum said, "Even in Buchenwald I was convinced that a regenerated Germany after the fall of the Nazis must have a chance to live and be a part of European society." Rejecting the plan of US Secretary of the Treasury Henry Morgenthau Jr to pastoralize Germany, closing down forever all but the lightest industry, Winston Churchill said, "You cannot indict a whole nation." Edmund Wilson warned, "Our whole world is poisoned now and we must realize that outlawing the enemy makes it easy to dislike one's allies."

As the dust of battle settled, people became travelers again. Werner Bischof and René Burri, feeling guilt at having lived the war in their impassive native Switzerland, set out separately for Germany, Bischof to take pictures of the ruins there and in the East, the younger Burri as a teenage bicyclist. "I still remember those smashed German cities, I had the feeling there would never be life again," he recalled. Simone de Beauvoir made her first visit to Switzerland and was relieved by its normality. "What a pleasure to have supper after the cinema," she wrote. "It reminds one of before the war."

The opening of frontiers meant that foreigners could look at one another again. A group of English hymn singers in Hyde Park seemed wonderfully exotic to Ernst Haas. "I was amazed by those faces, they couldn't be in Vienna." Inge Morath, by then a photographer as well as a writer, saw a lady sitting in a limousine as she walked toward Buckingham Palace and couldn't resist the shot.

"The chauffeur was about to kill me. So I apologized and said I'm so sorry. My English was so topsy-turvy and I said I am so sorry so much and she said what are you doing? and I said what are *you* doing? I am taking a breath of air, she said." The woman was Lady Nash, an Edwardian beauty who now made ends meet by presenting debutantes. "Seeing a good thing like a photographer, she then befriended me. She loved that picture. She was never without a hat."

At the Savoy in London, within weeks of the war's end, evening dress was again obligatory and over £1 million was placed in bets at the first postwar Derby. "Long ago in 1945 all the nice people in England were poor, allowing for exceptions," Muriel Spark wrote, later, in her novel *The Girls of Slender Means*.

Wartime had meant sacrifice and terrible sorrow; some had also found it quite thrilling. "It could be established roughly that the wicked had stayed and the good had gone," Elizabeth Bowen wrote of wartime London. "There was a diffused gallantry in the atmosphere, an unmarriedness. . . ." In 1946 she wrote that she and her contemporaries felt like "goldfish in a bowl of exhausted water." "How empty, how sickish, how senseless everything suddenly seems the moment war is over," Edmund Wilson wrote.

There was much to be grateful for but little to celebrate. Rations of cooking fats were halved, there were shortages of everything from beer to alarm clocks and hot water bottles. Bread was rationed for the first time in 1946. By 1948 rations were well below the wartime average. There were new treats such as whale steak (said to be nearly delicious with onions) and a barracuda-like fish from South Africa called snoek, which was not a success despite such government-issued recipes as *snoek piquante*. An American visiting London in 1946 was quite disturbed: "An old acquaintance confided to me that his underclothes were becoming extremely ragged and that he did not know where the coupons (as distinguished from the money) for his next pair of pajamas would come from," he noted earnestly. Edmund Wilson, dining with friends in a smart restaurant, was the only one to order duck. It tasted awful. Wilson later learned he had eaten crow.

Returning servicemen were issued a random assortment of clothes. Ronald Searle, after four years in the notorious Changi jail in Singapore, was given his demob suit in the summer of 1946. "It was sharp and quite wrong, like one of those Sunday suits one used to see in small villages, above dazzlingly buffed-up boots. Except that, unlike the village boys, one didn't feel good in it. I felt and looked hangdog and dog-eared, which was not at all useful to one who was about to seek fame and fortune and who needed all the confidence he could muster to face all those people who had not been isolated from the world for nearly four years."

The British Empire, which fifty years earlier had covered one-fourth of the earth's land surface, dwindled and slowly died. In this retreating world it was natural to look back: *Brideshead Revisited* came out in 1945 and so did John Betjeman's hymn to Miss Joan Hunter

Dunn, "The Subaltern's Love Song." Christopher Fry's romantic verse dramas enjoyed a vogue; well-dressed plays by Giraudoux and Anouilh were imported from France.

Morale needed a boost and in 1946 a terrific exhibition opened: "Britain Can Make It." Huge crowds gathered to look at 6,000 products, most of them marked "For export only." Nigel Dennis, ironic about British patience and obedience, put in his novel *Cards of Identity* a character with "the insanity of the phlegmatic, Britain-can-take-it type. He has gone on taking it so long that he no longer knows exactly what it is he is taking."

There was something exciting about leaving staunch, brave Britain for selfish, hedonistic France. Writing to her mother from Paris in September 1945, Nancy Mitford said, "I feel a totally different person as if I had come out of a coal mine into daylight."

Paris was just as cold and bleak but it was also better because the French cannot survive without decent food and a new fad. The food was tastier than in England thanks to a thriving black market — over one million people were engaged in it, a shocked American correspondent was told in 1946, though he was relieved to learn that most of them only worked at it part-time. And the new fad that everyone was talking about was Existentialism.

In 1945 Janet Flanner reported to *The New Yorker* that Jean-Paul Sartre was "the best known new Frenchman throughout Europe." He was, she added, automatically fashionable. "We mixed with *le tout Paris* at previews and premieres," Simone de Beauvoir wrote.

"A week never passed without the newspapers writing about us." It was the last time that French intellectuals would be international stars. De Beauvoir, thirty-seven years old in 1945, enjoyed the fame hugely, Sartre did not. "I don't even know what Existentialism is," he told the press. It didn't matter. The newspaper *La Croix* denounced it as a greater danger than eighteenth-century Rationalism or nineteenth-century Positivism. By the following spring reporters were tailing Sartre and De Beauvoir everywhere and breathlessly reported that the two were now going to the Hotel Pont Royal bar as well as to the Café de Flore. There were "Existentialist" nightclubs, such as the Tabou and La Rose Rouge, there was an "Existentialist" uniform, usually black and dingy, there were even "Existentialist" graffiti in the WCs of "Existentialist" hangouts: neither obscenities nor hearts pierced with arrows, but serious thoughts on nothingness, suicide and the Bikini atoll. Everyone came to St-Germain-des-Prés to join the new fad although Jacques Prévert, who lived in Montmartre, said of St-Germain-des-Prés, after its golden age had passed, "It was never a real quarter. It had neither peanut vendors nor whores."

On 3 May 1947, General de Gaulle, who had left power, held a press conference to describe the program of his political party, the RPF. The center of page one of *Samedi-Soir*, however, was taken up with a large photograph of two downcast young people who were identified as "two impoverished existentialists, Vadim and Gréco, exchanging depressing thoughts at the entrance to an existentialist *cave*."

The great Colette had De Beauvoir come around so

she could inspect her younger rival. "Do you like animals?" Colette inquired. "No," said De Beauvoir. Colette, she added, "stared me up and down with an Olympian gaze."

For Simone de Beauvoir it was a heady time. "Paris was still as intimate as a village." It was a moment of unity, but only a moment. "We all sang in chorus the hymn of our future," she wrote. The choristers would soon become rival soloists: when Sartre and Camus broke, it made headlines in *Samedi-Soir*.

The fuss over Existentialism, like the later fuss over the New Look, was easily explained by De Beauvoir: France had to defend herself by exporting traditional native products, fashion and literature, because she was now a second-rank power.

The eight-year conflict in Indochina against the forces of Ho Chi Minh, which began in 1946, cost 172,000 French casualties, further weakening a country which at the end of World War II had the oldest population of Europe. And France lacked Britain's moral confidence: unlike Britain, France had shamed herself in the war and her shame was often expressed in acts of arbitrary and self-serving revenge.

Within a few days of the Liberation a new column appeared in daily papers after Births, Deaths and Marriages. It was headed Arrests and Purges. *L'Epuration* was arguably the murkiest period of French history and accurate figures of those slain or sentenced are still not available. The French, always secretive and suspicious, became warier than ever: "There was a terrible discretion between friends, after years of separation, and not knowing what the friends had thought or done, or where they had been," Martha Gellhorn wrote.

Some were punished and others deserved to be, but the great monuments of French arts and letters — Picasso, Matisse, Braque, Cocteau, Gide — were still there and like monuments they had no artistic heirs with the exception of the film director Jean Renoir, who returned from the US in 1949 and whom François Truffaut called the father of the New Wave. The center of painting would move from the Ecole de Paris to New York: "The Frenchman has so much tradition that he can easily say anything except what he wants to say," said the American critic Harold Rosenberg. And in the next decade French writers, having seen the consequences of political commitment from the late 1930s to the Cold War, would turn inward: "Instead of being political, commitment for a writer means full awareness of the current problems of his own language, belief in the importance of these problems, and the will to resolve them from the inside," wrote the novelist Alain Robbe-Grillet.

The ever-supple Jean Cocteau, a Paris ornament before, during and after the Occupation, found the British Navy's duffle coat so chic that he started wearing one. Jean Genet, looking at huge, white-toothed GIs walking past the Rhumerie Martiniquaise on the boulevard St-Germain, declared that "these costumed civilians" had no style. The GIs had a warmer reception from Gertrude Stein, who had returned to Paris with the words, "Yes, it was the same, so much more beautiful, but it was the same."

Even Mistinguett returned briefly to the stage in

1949, making certain that her young chorus line was buttoned to the neck. In October 1945, General de Gaulle wrote to Jacques Maritain, his Ambassador to the Vatican, "When you left last December, the French were unhappy. Now they are discontented. That's progress." Shortly after, De Gaulle resigned the presidency, to return in 1958 when twenty-four highly combustible Fourth Republic governments had made it clear that only he could lead the country into order and out of the disastrous Algerian war.

Old France, with its nuanced elegance and splendor, tried to survive. Jacques Dumaine, the wise *chef de protocol* at the Quai d'Orsay — a man who described himself as a stoic with enthusiasm, a combination only *vieille France* could produce — went to a soirée at the house of the famous host Etiènne de Beaumont. "A huge Picasso had been installed between the gold and white 18th century *boiseries*," he wrote. "It doesn't shock because, except among human beings, one beauty is always pleased to be next to another."

In 1947 a young couturier named Christian Dior prepared for a new sort of beauty. The hideous fashions that French women wore during the war — the hats that were too large, the skirts that were too short, the shoes that were too heavy, the pompadours with hair trailing in the back — these hideous fashions, he explained in his memoirs, had been a form of defiance to the Vichy regime: "For lack of other materials, feathers and veils promoted to the dignity of flags floated through France like revolutionary banners." To reward this patriotism, Dior fashioned for women a New Look, sumptuously feminine, all curves and folds, rustling with the sound of taffeta, which some of the younger fashion editors had never heard. He showed his collection on 12 February 1947 and the success was so great that the queen of the "Existentialists," Juliette Gréco, came by to exchange her meaningful black for Dior's frills.

Many people, especially in austerity Britain, thought Dior's extravagant use of fabrics outrageous. "Paris forgets this is 1947," sniffed a headline in *Picture Post*, and Sir Stafford Cripps suggested the New Look be boycotted to save material. Even in prosperous America, there were outcries: "Out of one Paris model you can cut two American dresses."

France and America resumed their love-hate relationship. One conflict was over Coca-Cola, which had been sold in France since 1919 but which became a threat to civilization when *Le Monde* disclosed that Coca-Cola hoped to sell 240 million bottles a year to France. "Certain sound citizens," said *Le Monde*, evidently considering itself among them, "feel that since many French customs have already regrettably disappeared, those that persist should be defended. For now it is a question of the whole panorama and morale of French civilization."

While newspapers trumpeted and "Existentialists" jitterbugged, people whose ancestors had created France's famous standards of civilization found it hard simply to survive. The *bofs* (short for *beurre, œufs, fromages*), or profiteers, had done nicely enough, but in 1946 Jacques Dumaine called on two elderly ladies from the world of Proust: the Countess Greffulhe and her sister, the Countess Ghislaine de Caraman-Chimay.

12

The courtyard of the house on the rue d'Astorg was an ensemble of balconies and perrons and colonnades as fabulous as Angkor Wat, Dumaine wrote. He followed a servant through room upon empty room to end in a very small one where the two ladies huddled around a coal stove. "They didn't plunge into their memories or express disenchantment. The precariousness of the present interests them more than their comfortable past. They talked without sadness of their childhood house on the quai Malaquais and never mentioned friends who had died. They speak only of the future: they live."

In the spring of 1947, in the restaurant of the Museum of Modern Art in New York, a tableful of photographers and their friends talked about founding a cooperative agency. The founding photographers were Henri Cartier-Bresson, Robert Capa, David Seymour, George Rodger and William Vandivert. Vandivert soon dropped out and Rodger spent most of his time working in Africa and Asia, so the first three became the nucleus of the agency which was called, after the double bottle of champagne, Magnum.

Inevitably, Magnum's nerve center was Paris and Capa its president and chief fixer. Already famous for his Spanish Civil War pictures and for his daredevil courage as a photographer in World War II (he took five parachute jumps, his first, in one day to qualify as an instant paratrooper), Capa had, said his friend Irwin Shaw, the thick-lashed eyes of a street poet or a Neapolitan urchin. He was a ladykiller and a man's man —

"Everyone loved him so much that no one could envy him," said the writer Peter Viertel — and he spoke many languages with an accent his friends called Capanese. "Cookie," Capa said to Don Cook, then a neophyte newsman, "only a Hungarian knows how to misuse English correctly."

A naturalized American, Capa was born André Friedmann in Budapest. He came to Paris in 1933 and claimed to be the assistant of a famous American photographer, Robert Capa. The work of "Capa" was soon sufficiently in demand for Robert Capa to come into existence. Cartier-Bresson always called him André.

Magnum settled into a building at 125 rue du Faubourg St Honoré, about ten minutes from the Hotel Lancaster where Capa got his racing tips. Next to the office was a café with a pinball machine which Capa played expertly. "Whenever he wanted to give you hell about lousy pictures or a story not well done, he took you down to the pinball machine," Erich Lessing says. Capa usually won.

"He was the man," Inge Morath says of Capa. "He was immensely funny, he was, I think, the most generous person I have ever known and he loved us. He said you're my horses, my racehorses. He was also selfish and boasting and all that, but he was just simply wonderful."

Capa cadged scarce film from American pals and gave out assignments in a most personal style. Erich Lessing, a Viennese who had lived in Israel as a carp breeder, beach photographer and taxi driver before joining the Associated Press and then Magnum in 1950, says: "I was in Turkey doing photographs for the Marshall Plan when I got a cable from Capa saying

13

Locust invasion Persia. You have Life assignment. Go. I finally got a visa and went. I only found out afterwards that we didn't have a *Life* assignment, that Capa had said if Erich comes back with some pictures I'll get him into *Life.*

"Then I had an idea for a story on Germany. He said okay, do it, but you need some backing. You have a *Look* assignment. I said how come I have a *Look* assignment? He said, if I tell you you have a *Look* assignment, you have a *Look* assignment. I had a *Look* assignment."

Inge Morath and Ernst Haas arrived together from Vienna on Bastille Day, 1949, and went off to show revelers in St-Germain-des-Prés how to dance a Viennese waltz, including the reverse. They had been a well-known magazine team in Vienna. "I didn't know about taking pictures. I was very intellectually brought up, I didn't know it was something you did in good conscience," Morath says. Capa had invited Haas and Werner Bischof to join Magnum in 1949 (Morath was invited to join in 1952).

Haas and Bischof were very different and became close friends. "Haas came from war-torn Vienna and was longing for aesthetics, Werner was trained by the Bauhaus and was longing for real life," Bischof's widow, Rosellina, says. "Growing up in Switzerland in the war was like being in a hothouse and when Werner came out he was all sensitivity. The first trip he made to Germany, in 1945, he was crushed."

"I loved Bischof very much," says Haas. "He was an aesthete, a poet, a knight." Before starting on a story, Bischof always made careful notes and sketches. "Cartier-Bresson admired Werner because he was al-ways drawing. At that time we didn't know that painting was Henri's passion," says Rosellina Bischof, who married René Burri after Bischof's death.

Everyone was at the right age to have a wonderful time and the world was ripe for fun. The photographers were spirited although usually poor and cold. "I always had newspaper in my shoes," Inge Morath says. "I gave up that habit late, I got so used to it. It's quite cosy." They lived in cheap hotels — the small rooms at the top, which were always too hot or too cold — and from time to time, with Capa, they mixed with people who were glamorous and grand.

"In the late 50s you stopped feeling innocent about owning things, but before there was a marvelous period," Inge Morath says. "I never wanted a Cadillac, but to ride in one was great. To get a fur coat, any fur coat, was cheap. Or smoking — there were things that you simply thought were wonderful and that you did not discuss. Or diets. I never heard anyone talk about diets. Everyone was hungry and therefore relatively thin. We were a bunch of gypsies, street photographers, it didn't matter where you'd go or when you came back. We needed very little money and the intellectual excitement was immense." Most of them used small cameras with rangefinders. "It was a different kind of photography with rangefinders," Morath says. "It was a time when people felt good about being photo-reporters, before it all became art."

The photographers often edited each other's contact sheets. "I edited Henri's because he trusted me," Morath says, "I did it for Haasi. Later, we still did it one for the other, which was excellent. I tell you the atmo-

14

sphere was quite wonderful. And then we had some Americans. There was always a stray pretty American girl or two. Then slowly they started to hire editors. It started with the cousins of Capa, he had endless cousins, but then also there came the professional people. Some were fierce, some were less fierce."

Capa was not one to discuss his problems but his passport had been taken away in the McCarthy period for reasons that were never specified and he was unable to travel. Finally he got back his passport, and it seems likely that he took on his last assignment to pay his legal fees. According to his brother, Cornell, in the spring of 1954 Capa went to Tokyo for an exhibition of his work and to photograph children for a Japanese magazine. While he was there *Life* asked him to go to Vietnam to replace a photographer who had been given compassionate leave because his mother was ill. Capa went and on 25 May 1954, about fifty miles south of Hanoi, he stepped on a mine having earlier announced, "This is going to be a beautiful story. I shall be on my best behavior today. I shall not insult people. I shall not even mention the excellence of my work." He was killed instantly, aged forty. The French awarded a posthumous Croix de Guerre and among the wreaths was one from a Hanoi restaurant where Capa had terrified the waiters, charmed the hostess and taught the bartender to mix a decent dry martini. The wreath was inscribed, "A notre ami."

Magnum didn't know it at the time, but Werner Bischof had died nine days earlier in a car accident in the Andes. "I lost Capa and Werner in an hour," Haas says. Telegrams announcing the two deaths arrived almost simultaneously in Egypt, where he was on assignment.

David Seymour took over, announcing the news in a letter that began, "My Dear Magnum Family." When she first heard the name David Seymour, Inge Morath had imagined a languid English aristocrat. Seymour was actually a plump and owlish Polish Jew whose real name was David Szymin and who was always called "Chim." Unlike the extrovert Capa, he was scholarly, worried, gentle. He wore a suit and a tie. "Chim picked up his camera the way a doctor takes his stethoscope out of his bag," Cartier-Bresson has said, "applying his diagnosis to the condition of the heart; his own was vulnerable." Chim's photographs of children are astonishing in their affection and tact: he caught all war in one picture of a little girl with a very large bow in her hair and a baffled look in her eye who is making a frightful scrawl on the blackboard where she had been asked to draw her home. Chim was a bachelor and, wrote Cartier-Bresson, a natural godfather.

He was also an expert eater and, like Capa, he knew everyone. "He had connections with the glamorous world everywhere, he even had connections with the Pope," says René Burri. Whereas the others had been recruited by Capa, Burri was taken on by Chim. It seemed very easy, at first. "Then he called me and said, 'Go to Egypt, Nasser has taken the canal.' I smuggled my film out of Egypt via a Swissair pilot and it got delayed. Chim started screaming. The pictures were lost for three days. Then came the comeuppance. He said, 'I don't care. You walk, you swim, you crawl. You don't miss a deadline.'"

From 1955 Burri tried to become a full member of Magnum. "In 1958 Henri said you're not ready yet and I went to South America for six months. Today we still get a little too hard about new members, but I think it's good. Magnum is a vulnerable club. Sometimes people just come in and take. I gritted my teeth and said I'll show them and I did my best work after they turned me down the last time." He was accepted in 1959.

In 1956 Chim went to cover the aborted Anglo-French Suez invasion. "I talked to Chim on the telephone in Nicosia just ten days earlier and I said to him please don't go," Erich Lessing says. "It's stupid, it makes no sense, it's not going to work out, don't go."

"We'd had enough deaths, you know, and I thought the whole thing made no sense. So why get into a crossfire, it was a badly organized story from all sides. But Chim desperately wanted to do it, physically he wanted to prove to himself and to everybody else that he could do the same things as Capa. It didn't work out." Chim fell under Egyptian machine-gun fire on 10 November 1956, ten days before his forty-fifth birthday.

The sorrow after three deaths was so awful that Haas left Magnum for a while. The same year, Lessing went through a great personal crisis when he covered the Hungarian uprising. He was a natural choice: he knew Eastern Europe intimately and was friendly with politicians in many countries, including Hungary. Budapest marked an end for him: "I did not want to cover any revolutions or any wars any more. It makes no sense, I've seen too much."

To Lessing, the failure of the Hungarian revolution was also the failure of photo-journalism: "I had thought, Capa said so too, that by taking pictures we were showing what the world is like, that you can at least in a small way influence behavior and the course of politics. But every journalist in a shorter or longer time knows this is not true — the most horrible war pictures will never end wars. By showing revolution you do not help the revolution nor do you do the contrary, you just document it. I'm not even so sure — though it would be anathema to say it — that it's so important to document it because that doesn't change anything and I'm not sure that a document that doesn't change anything is a valid document."

The whole world followed Russia's repression of the Hungarian Revolution. The French heard on their radios, "We are now going off the air. *Vive l'Europe. Vive La France.* We are dying for freedom." And then silence. Budapest brought the Cold War into the living room and blew up any remaining hopes for a post-Stalin liberalization of the satellite countries.

Ten years before Budapest, in 1946, the Soviet Union had established control over Eastern Europe. In 1948 came the Prague coup and the probable murder of Jan Masaryk. The following year saw both the formation of NATO and the explosion of a Russian nuclear bomb. East and West seemed headed for confrontation: after the Prague coup General Lucius D. Clay, the US Military Governor in Germany, had expressed his fear that "war could break out with dramatic suddenness."

16

In France, Jacques Dumaine at the Quai d'Orsay was disturbed that his country seemed so little concerned with the possibility of war: "We don't bother to look at the uncontrolled and perhaps inevitable danger for the rest of the world of the rivalry between the United States and the Soviet Union. . . . We are at the present time the least lugubrious of mortals." Theodore H. White understood European passivity very well: "The United States and Russia constantly want to act, to do, to make history — and Europe has had a bellyful of history."

As Janet Flanner foresaw in 1946, "The earth's surface is changing. Europe is contracting; the USSR and USA areas of influence are expanding. It is as if Europe were slowly entering a new ice age."

The ice age struck literally in the winter of 1947, one of the coldest in history. "If 1946 was *Annus Mirabilis*," Britain's Chancellor of the Exchequer, Hugh Dalton, said, "1947 was *Annus Horrendus*."

The awfulness of *Annus Horrendus* and the spreading chill of the Cold War helped to bring about with amazing speed that which Europe wanted most: recovery.

The bad winter put Britain in such financial straits that in February 1947 it informed the United States that within weeks it would be obliged to end its aid to Greece. The United States took over. In March, the Truman Doctrine was proclaimed. In June, at Harvard's commencement, Secretary of State George C. Marshall outlined what would later be called the "Marshall Plan." The Soviet Union, which had been invited to participate in the plan, rejected and later opposed it. The plan — according to Truman, Marshall blushed when he was told it would be named for him — was an immediate success. Of the $17 billion approved for its use by Congress, only $13 billion was needed — an almost unique example of official underspending.

If recovery was swifter than expected, it was partly because of West Germany's *Wirtschaftswunder*, or economic miracle. The Marshall Plan gave Germany $4.5 billion in aid, but a steelmaker later informed William Manchester, author of *The Arms of Krupp*, "Marshall had little to do with it. This was a German miracle."

The single most important event in the miracle was the German currency reform of 20 June 1948, engineered by Ludwig Erhard in Trizonia, the Ruritanian name the British, French and Americans had given to the amalgam of their occupation zones. On currency reform day, the old Reichsmark was no longer legal tender and ten old Reichsmarks could be exchanged for one new Deutschemark (the rate was later reduced to 6.5 DMs for 100 old marks). "The results were dramatic," Richard Mayne writes. "Savings were wiped out — but so were illusions. . . . With everyone called back to about the same starting-line, a new race for prosperity began." It was a brutal competition with no room for the weak.

The French novelist Michel Tournier, who was studying at Tübingen, saw the overnight change: "On Sunday, 20 June, as if struck by a magic wand, towns came to life, markets displayed their goods, shopwindows overflowed with merchandise. Ration cards were abolished and with them the inevitable black market. . . . This sudden change . . . to a savagely free economy dominated solely by the law of lucre created numberless victims, all the lame ducks who had been vegetating in a penury equal for all. But the whiplash it gave to production had spectacular results."

The fortunes of war caused many of West Germany's outmoded factories to be destroyed or dismantled, but stocks of useful heavy machine tools were intact. The GNP rose by seventy percent in five years' time. For every new house built in France, the Germans built eight. On 3 February 1951, the steelmaker and convicted war criminal Alfried Krupp was released from prison after serving half his sentence. He was greeted like a returning hero and within a short time was again considered the richest man in Europe.

Not all Germany was so fortunate. The Russians reacted to the currency reform with the Berlin blockade. The blockade, broken by an airlift of the Western allies, produced an important psychological change: for British, French and American soldiers, the West Germans were no longer "they." They became "we."

Berlin was an island, cut off from the rest of the country's prosperity and the recipient of such subsidies as the *Notopfer Berlin*, a stamp Germans were obliged to put on letters in addition to normal postage as a sacrifice for Berlin. Berlin was the one city in Germany with no eye to the future: it was a place of memory. It built a *Teufelsberg* (or devil's mountain) out of rubble while other cities were building skyscrapers, and as a reminder it left unrepaired the bomb-damaged tower of the Kaiser Wilhelm Memorial Church. Berlin, famous for its sharp and gritty humor, Berlin which had referred to Goering as Hermann Meyer because of his statement,

"If an enemy plane ever crosses our border you can call me Meyer" — Berlin knew it was an island and Berliners cheekily referred to themselves as *Die Insulaner*, the name of a popular satiric radio program. But Berlin was tired and tattered, a city for the old: the young had moved on to brighter places where memory was no burden.

Other cities shone in the 1950s with glassy skyscrapers, housing projects and new schools. Le Corbusier, usually underemployed in France, built both a housing project in Marseilles and the chapel at Ronchamp, near Besançon. Italy produced not only exciting buildings but also, thanks to a new breed of industrial designers and enlightened manufacturers, stunning typewriters and motorbikes and sewing machines. There was the sound of jackhammers and also, everywhere, the reviving sound of music. In one year, 1951, Bayreuth reopened, *The Rake's Progress* had its premiere in Venice and Maria Callas made her La Scala debut.

Although poverty in Italy's *mezzogiorno* region was still terrible, the country's industrial growth between 1950 and 1958 was an impressive nine percent annually. The *Autostrada del Sol* suggested a route to joy simply by its name, the *Topolino* (Mickey Mouse) motorcar may have been tiny but it had a wonderful jaunty charm. Italy even struck oil, guided by the swashbuckling Enrico Mattei, and by 1958 was supplying nearly seventy percent of Europe's natural gas. The Italian political scene seemed to other Europeans robustly unscrupulous (everyone knew about the priest who told his flock that while Stalin couldn't see into the voting booth, God could). By the mid 1950s *La Dolce Vita* was on its way.

In England, the doughty Britain-Can-Make-It spirit was drowned in the sheer larkiness of the 1951 Festival of Britain, which included a fun fair, an eccentrics' corner and a permanent structure, the Royal Festival Hall. "I don't think it's a particularly wonderful building," Frank Lloyd Wright remarked, "but I think it's wonderful that your country has a new building."

Britain had many new buildings, in fact, but recovery was slow and austerity still cast its dreary pall. Inge Morath continued to bring fresh French eggs on visits to London and the memory of meager repasts lasted so long that in 1972, Judy Montagu, a friend of Princess Margaret, was identified in her obituary as "the first person who realized that the war was actually over. To a society numb with austerity she introduced avocado pears, gossip and real Americans." At the Coronation of Elizabeth II in 1953 there was a question of whether ox-roasting would be allowed since rationing was still on. It was.

The degree of recovery that the United Nations predicted for 1959 had already occurred in Europe by 1952, only seven years after the war. Britain was among the slowest nations to recover but even so she was enjoying unparalleled economic growth and in absolute terms was richer by the 1950s than at any other time in her history. Prime Minister Harold Macmillan, adapting Eisenhower's punchy phrase, could truly say, "Most of our people have never had it so good."

A new materialism was born. Lady Docker and her gold-plated Daimler were gossip-column regulars while Joe Lampton of John Braine's novel *Room at the Top*, claimed, "I wanted an Aston Martin, I wanted a three-guinea linen shirt, I wanted a girl with a Riviera suntan — these were my rights." Scampi and garlic entered English cuisine and eighty-three-year-old Somerset Maugham, who came up to the Dorchester from the Riviera in 1957, found there were no crumpets for tea. "When I was younger one could have crumpets and muffins for tea," he complained. "One cannot any more in this hard life we lead."

In Paris, even Simone de Beauvoir was pleased by her new affluence. "Since 1954 my books earn me a great deal of money; in 1952 I bought myself an automobile and in 1955 an apartment," she wrote in *La Force des Choses*. In the bitter winter of 1953–54, she noted that middle-class ladies were giving cast-offs to Abbé Pierre, who had founded a mission for the poor and homeless.

In 1950 the first Club Méditerranée opened and in the same year France again became Europe's largest tourist country with three million visitors, many of them Americans baffled by "Yank, go home" signs. In 1955 France brought out the Citroën DS, a car as sleek and streamlined as any *belle Américaine*, though — mistrustful of modernity — Citroën gave out a hand crank with each car. In 1956 Simone de Beauvoir read *The Lonely Crowd*, *The Exurbanites* and *The Organization Man*, evidently with the thought that it can't happen here. It could, and did.

Germany was doing best of all, drinking five times as much champagne as before the war and eating twenty-five million pounds of caviar a year. "In Germany," said a writer, "prosperity is the solution of every problem."

In an article called "What Shall We Tell Our Children?" Günter Grass asked his compatriots to look beyond their prosperity and to remember: the Germans' economic success, he argued, "cannot conceal the moral vacuum engendered by their incomparable guilt."

By the mid 1950s, one Western European in twenty-five had a motorcar and over thirty million traveled on the Continent during vacations — about the same number as had struggled across it as refugees a decade earlier. Ideologically, the divisions between Left and Right had hardened with the Korean war and with the rush of spies and defectors — Bruno Pontecorvo, Klaus Fuchs, Burgess and Maclean, all in the years 1950–51 — which gave fuel to the ambitions of Senator Joseph McCarthy and his "anti-communist" witch hunts. In Vicenza, in June 1953, Simone de Beauvoir saw a headline, "I Rosenberg Sono Stati Assassinati."

Prosperity was wonderful, but there was great insecurity and a nagging suspicion that the brave ideals of 1945 had been tainted. In 1958, Aldous Huxley worried about the perils of overorganization: "A new ethic is replacing our traditional ethical system — the system in which the individual is primary. The key words in this Social Ethics are 'adjustment,' 'adaptation,' 'socially oriented behavior.'. . . Its basic assumption is that the social whole has greater worth and significance than its individual parts."

There was no room left for Huxley's old-fashioned humanism, and the Welfare State, in whatever form it took throughout Europe, provided greater equality, opportunity and security than people had ever known. In 1957 the Common Market came to life with the signing of the Treaty of Rome. The time had come for planned economies, planned towns, planned births. *Le planning* became a French word and so, in time, did *le stress*.

Europe had been rejuvenated, which is not at all the same thing as being young. Those who were young could not admire what their parents had built or share what they had suffered: they only knew that they were living in an uneasy world. Rebellion came later; in the 50s the young were merely "alienated," "the silent generation." The so-called Angry Young Men turned out not to be very young or very angry: what counted then, and what lasts now, is rock 'n' roll. In Paris, those in the know deserted the genteel pseudo-Dixieland of St-Germain-des-Prés for the raucous jukebox of Al's GI's Paradise off the Rond Point des Champs-Elysées, and teenagers everywhere found that for the price of a disc they could share a common language and a common style. Style was important. In 1957 Thom Gunn wrote a poem, "Elvis Presley:"

He turns revolt into a style, prolongs
The impulse to a habit of the time.

With the youth culture came *And God Created Woman*, a film dedicated to pleasure and directed by the former dispirited "Existentialist" Roger Vadim. It made Brigitte Bardot famous. More than that, it made her significant. Simone de Beauvoir wrote a book about her and Diana Vreeland proclaimed, "Just as Mick Jagger, for me, *was* the creature for the Sixties, Bardot *was* the creature for the Fifties. She prepared the way for the

Sixties and she made the Sixties alluring rather than just ugly. Her lips made Mick Jagger's lips *possible*."

Pop sociology was another sign of the times, for the times — although nominally still the 50s — had become today. Postwar was over; all the ingredients of the present time were onstage, from hip replacements to battery hens to nuclear terror. In 1952 the World Health Organization sent out its first warning about smoking and lung cancer, in 1955 Dr Spock's book on baby care came to Europe, in 1958 John Kenneth Galbraith published *The Affluent Society*, and in 1959 the first American advisors were killed in Vietnam.

Each person has a clear memory of when postwar ended and today began. For Ernst Haas it was in the early 1950s when he began taking the color photographs for which he is famous. "I would like to do black and white again," he says, "but one of the reasons I went into color is because it made a distinction between the grayness of one period and the life that came later." For Inge Morath the postwar period ended on the day in 1959 when for the first time there were so many cars on her Paris street that she was unable to park. She sold her car, a gray Peugeot that she had bought from a cousin of Cartier-Bresson.

In 1958 came the Brussels World's Fair, billed as the greatest show Europe had seen since the war and a tremendous success with forty-eight participating countries and forty-nine million visitors. Like so much else, the Fair was a Cold War event with vast and competing Russian and American pavilions (the Russians brought Sputnik and even the space dog Laika), but it was also all that a World's Fair should be — full of excitement and hope. Henri Cartier-Bresson photographed the Fair and sensed the hope. He also felt wary because, he says, photography is a way of feeling the pulse, of sensing things in advance: it is as if the photographer sniffed smoke in the air and later there was a blazing fire.

"In the Fifties," Cartier-Bresson says, "the world had been totally changed by scientific discoveries made during the war. These technological changes became a part of our lives, creating deeper and deeper tensions so that we are in a world that seems headed for suicide."

The photographer's whiff of smoke hangs in the air still, but in 1958 no one noticed and the theme of the Fair was, "For a more human world."

Mary Blume
Paris, 1984

1 Werner Bischof *In the ruins of Warsaw* 1947

2 Robert Capa
The Liberation of Paris
25 August 1944

3 Robert Capa *Pablo Picasso in his studio, rue des Grands-Augustins, Paris 1944*

4 Henri Cartier-Bresson *Jean-Paul Sartre (with glasses) at auction of illustrated books, Paris 1944*

5 Ernst Haas *Piccadilly, London* 1947

6 Ernst Haas *Returning prisoner of war, Vienna* 1945

7 Henri Cartier-Bresson
*Deported Russians
leaving Germany for home* 1945

8 Werner Bischof *Mother and child, Warsaw* 1948

9 Robert Capa *German family sheltering in foxhole 1945*

10 Henri Cartier-Bresson
*Deported Russians leaving
Germany for home* 1945

11 Henri Cartier-Bresson *Lining up for food in front of Paris shop* 1945

12 Henri Cartier-Bresson *Simone de Beauvoir* 1946

13 Werner Bischof *Prisoners of war in the French sector of Vienna* 1945

14 Henri
Cartier-Bresson
Hamburg 1953

15 David Seymour *Prostitute in Essen* 1947

16 Robert Capa *Organ grinder, Berlin* 1945

17 David Seymour *Vienna* 1948

18 Werner Bischof *Reconstruction in the Vercors, France 1945*

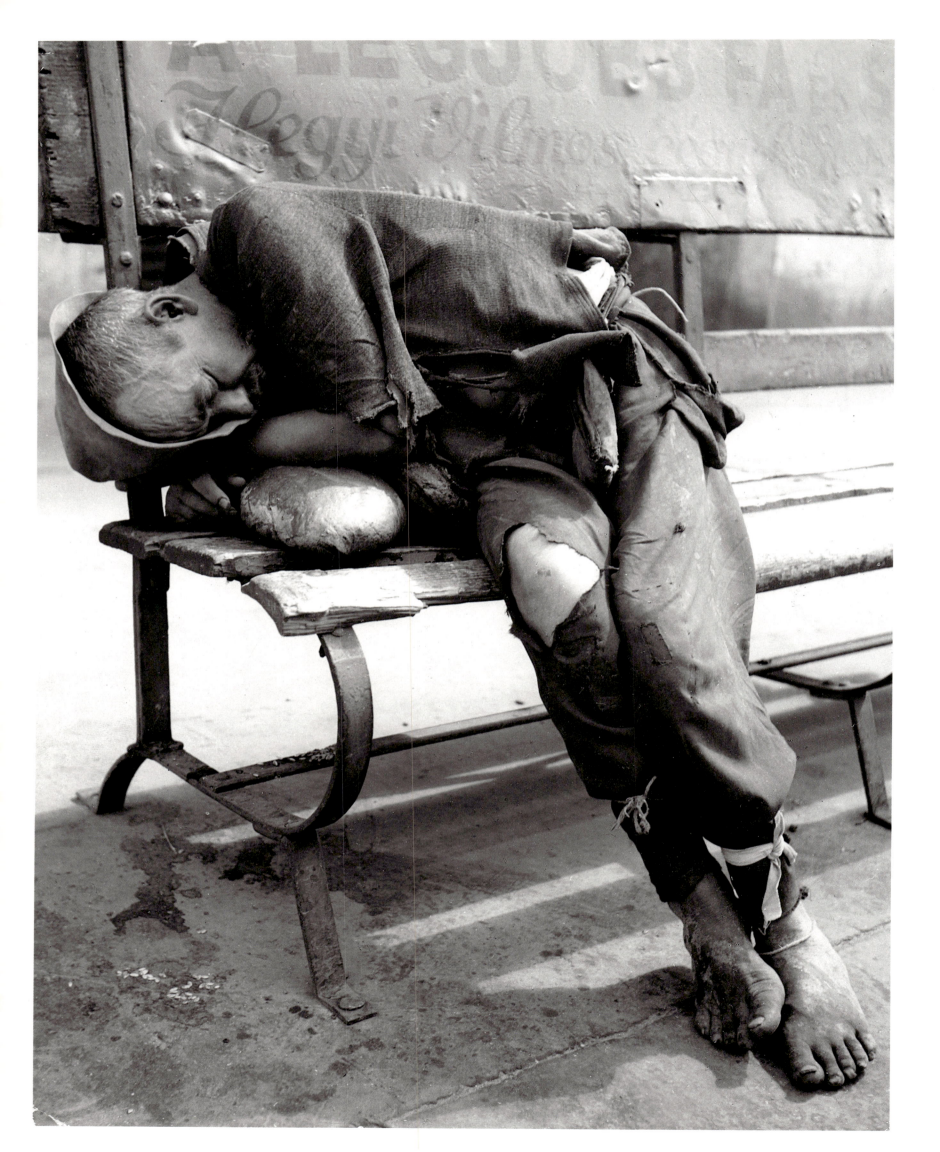

19 Werner Bischof
Bucharest 1947

20 Werner Bischof
Verona 1950

22 David Seymour
*Mother and children,
Naples* 1948

23 Werner Bischof *Sleeping it off, Warsaw* 1947

24 Werner Bischof *Farmers in Hungary* 1948

27 David Seymour *Orphanage, Greece* 1953

28 David Seymour *Begging child and American sailors, Naples* 1948

29 David Seymour *UNESCO literacy program in Calabria, Italy* 1950

30 David Seymour *Disturbed orphan drawing her home, Poland* 1948

31 David Seymour *Russian soldiers in the Prater, Vienna 1949*

32 Elliott Erwitt
Eiffel Tower reflection,
Paris 1950

33 Erich Lessing *Frankfurt* 1951

34 Henri
Cartier-Bresson
*Aquila degli Abruzzi,
Italy* 1952

35 Erich Lessing *Königsallee, Düsseldorf* 1955

36 Elliott Erwitt *Rome* 1951

37 David Seymour *Beach near Travemünde, Germany, overlooking the Russian zone 1949*

38 Henri Cartier-Bresson *Scheveningen, Holland* 1953

39 Werner Bischof *London* 1950

40 Henri Cartier-Bresson *Venice* 1952

41 Henri Cartier-Bresson *Henri Matisse at his home in Vence, France 1944*

42 David Seymour *Peggy Guggenheim on the Grand Canal, Venice 1950*

43 David Seymour
*Coca-Cola delivery,
Venice* 1951

44 Henri
Cartier-Bresson
*Porter's lodge,
Barcelona* 1952

45 Robert Capa *The New Look, Paris* 1947

46 Henri Cartier-Bresson *Christian Dior with client* 1950

47 Werner Bischof *Street in Montmartre, Paris* 1950

48 Henri Cartier-Bresson *Georges Braque* 1950

49 Henri Cartier-Bresson
Coronation shop window,
London 1952

50 Elliott Erwitt *Paris café* 1952

51 Henri Cartier-Bresson *Shop front, Dublin* 1952

52 Henri Cartier-Bresson *Academician en route to ceremony, Paris 1952*

53 Henri Cartier-Bresson *Changing of the guard, London 1952*

54 David Seymour *Naples* 1950

55 Marc Riboud *Organ grinder, London* 1954

56 Elliott Erwitt *Odessa, USSR* 1957

57 Elliott Erwitt *Valencia, Spain* 1951

58 Henri Cartier-Bresson
Brighton, England 1952

59 Henri Cartier-Bresson
Venice 1952

60 Werner Bischof *Paris* 1950

61 Ernst Haas *Paris* 1950

62 Henri Cartier-Bresson
At the races,
Prix de Paris 1951

63 Henri Cartier-Bresson
Scanno, Italy 1951

64 Henri Cartier-Bresson *At the races, Angers, France* 1953

65 Robert Capa *At the races, Deauville, France* 1952

66 Henri Cartier-Bresson
The Ascot train,
Waterloo Station, London 1953

67 Henri Cartier-Bresson *Spreading the gospel at Ascot, England* 1953

68 Ernst Haas *Sunday singers in Hyde Park, London 1947*

69 Robert Capa *London pub* 1951

70 Henri Cartier-Bresson *Flower sellers, London* 1953

overleaf:
71 David Seymour *Umbria, Italy* 1951

72 David Seymour *Umbria, Italy* 1951

73 Marc Riboud
*Peasant demonstration
near Bordeaux* 1953

74 Marc Riboud
Les Halles, Paris 1953

75 Henri Cartier-Bresson *Unemployed worker, Hamburg* 1952

76 Henri Cartier-Bresson *Port workers, Hamburg* 1952

77 David Seymour
Political rally, Florence 1953

78 Marc Riboud
Demonstration by dockers,
London 1954

79 Henri Cartier-Bresson *Duisburg, Germany 1955*

80 Erich Lessing
Railroad workers,
Poland 1956

81 Werner Bischof *Port of London* 1950

82 Henri Cartier-Bresson *The bridge at Tancarville, France, under construction* 1955

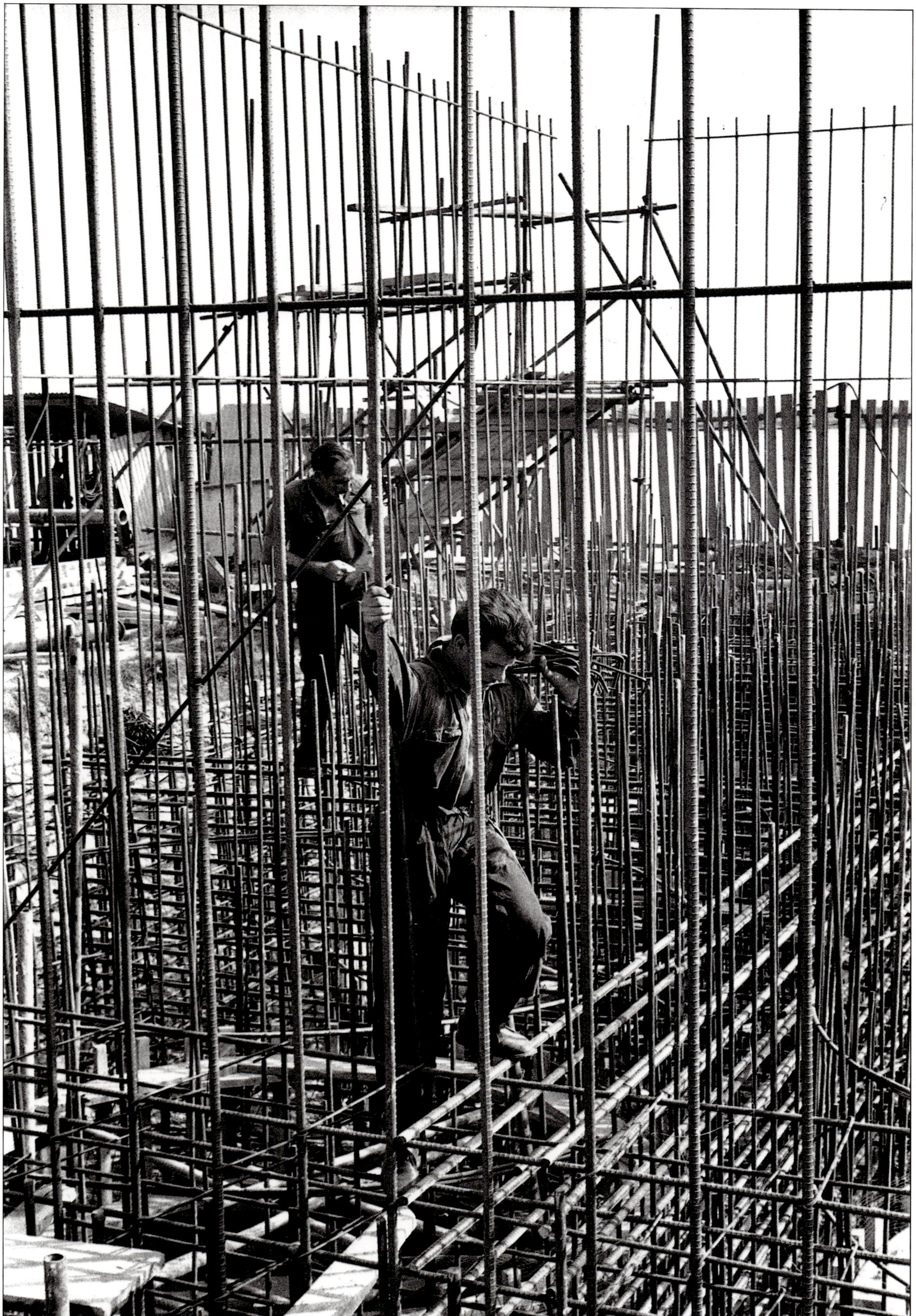

83 Ernst Haas *Scanning the news, Rome* 1948

84 Henri Cartier-Bresson *At the Salon des Arts ménagers, Paris 1953*

85 Henri Cartier-Bresson *Seminary students, near Burgos, Spain* 1953

86 Inge Morath *Holy Week, Seville* 1954

87 David Seymour *Archbishop Montini (later Pope Paul VI), Milan 1955*

88 David Seymour *Good Friday procession, Sicily* 1955

89 Marc Riboud *Notre Dame, Paris* 1953

90 René Burri *Pompeii* 1956

91 Henri Cartier-Bresson *The Serpentine, Hyde Park, London* 1945

92 Henri Cartier-Bresson *Bruges, Belgium* 1953

93 Inge Morath *Bond Street, London* 1954

94 Inge Morath *Bond Street, London* 1954

95 Robert Capa
Boulevard St-Michel,
Paris 1954

96 Inge Morath
*Beauty and the Beast
contest, Paris 1954*

97 Inge Morath *Left Bank café, Paris* 1954

98 Henri Cartier-Bresson *The news from Dien Bien Phu, Paris* 1954

99 Cornell Capa *Winchester School tailor, England* 1951

100 Marc Riboud *"Teddy boys," London* 1954

101 Henri Cartier-Bresson
Switzerland 1953

102 Erich Lessing
Czechoslovakia 1956

103 Elliott Erwitt
Paris 1949

104 Henri Cartier-Bresson
*Canal at Bougival,
near Paris 1955*

105 Henri Cartier-Bresson *Derby Day at Epsom, England* 1953

106 Henri Cartier-Bresson *Bullring at Pamplona, Spain* 1952

107 René Burri *Village of Trogen, Switzerland* 1956

108 Henri Cartier-Bresson *San Remo, Italy* 1953

109 Inge Morath
Mrs Evelyn Nash 1954

110 Marc Riboud
Hyde Park,
London 1954

111 Marc Riboud
St James's Park,
London 1954

112 Marc Riboud
Covent Garden, London 1955

113 Marc Riboud
Regent Street, London 1955

114 Henri Cartier-Bresson
Swimming in the Seine,
near Paris 1955

115 Henri Cartier-Bresson
Quai on the Seine,
Paris 1955

116 Erich Lessing *Tractor station at Karzag, Hungary 1956*   117 Henri Cartier-Bresson *Avenue du Maine, Paris 1954*

118 Marc Riboud
View from the National Hotel,
Moscow 1960

119 Henri Cartier-Bresson *View from Notre Dame, Paris* 1955

120 Henri Cartier-Bresson *Lisbon* 1955

123 Henri Cartier-Bresson
Champ de Mars,
Paris 1954

PAMIATKA
z JASNEJ GÓRY
CZESTOCHOWA
1956.

124 Erich Lessing
Czestochowa,
Poland 1956

125 David Seymour *Naples* 1956

126 Erich Lessing *Vienna* 1954

127 Erich Lessing
*Hungarian uprising,
Budapest 1956*

128 Erich Lessing
*Hungarian uprising,
Budapest* 1956

129 Erich Lessing *Russian tanks in Budapest* 1956

130 René Burri *Hungarian refugees arriving in Switzerland* 1956

131 René Burri *Czechoslovakia* 1957

132 René Burri *East German soldiers at Russian War Memorial, East Berlin* 1959

133 David Seymour
Arturo Toscanini 1954

134 Henri Cartier-Bresson *Colette and her maid* 1952

135 David Seymour *Maria Callas* 1956

136 David Seymour *Bernard Berenson at the Borghese Gallery, Rome 1955*

137 René Burri *At a Brancusi exhibition, the Kunsthaus, Zurich 1954*

138 Henri Cartier-Bresson *Milles Museum, Stockholm* 1956

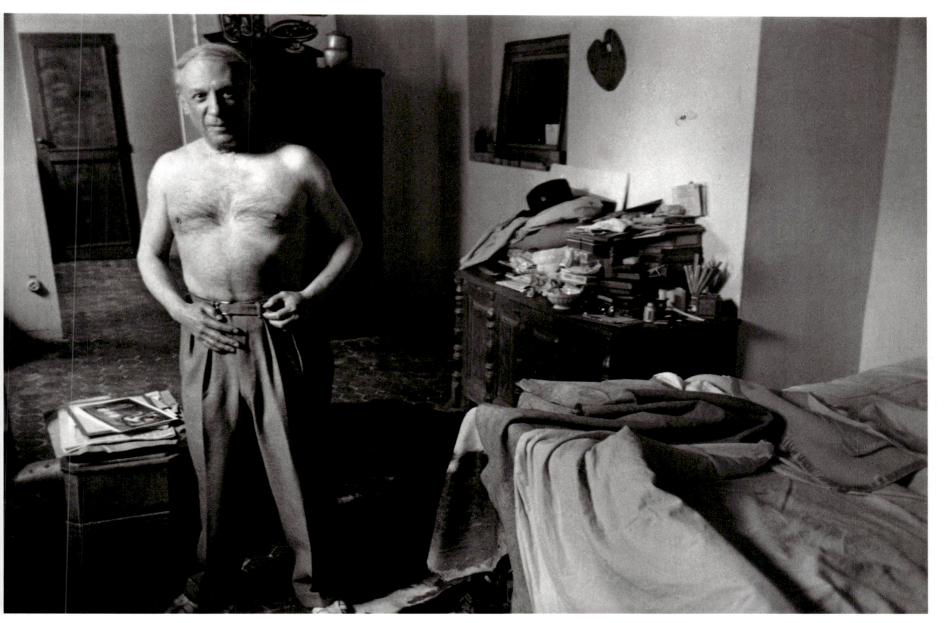

139 Henri Cartier-Bresson *Pablo Picasso at home, rue des Grands-Augustins, Paris* 1944

140 Inge Morath *Henry Moore in his studio* 1954

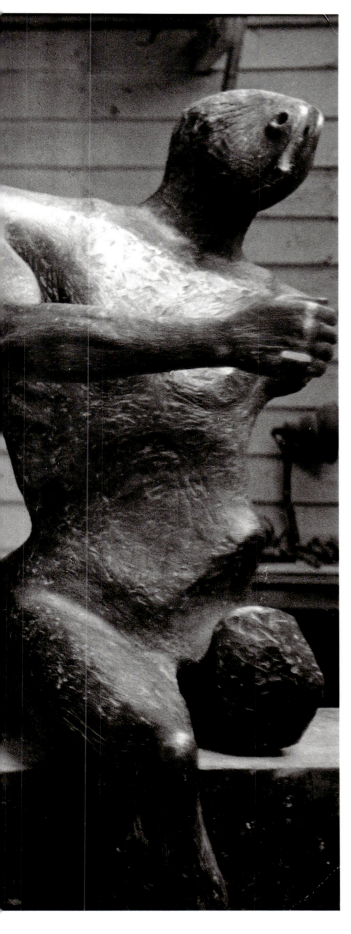

141 David Seymour *Naples* 1950

142 Henri Cartier-Bresson
Alberto Giacometti 1960

143 Burt Glinn
Bernard Buffet 1958

144 Henri Cartier-Bresson
Jacques Tati 1958

145 Henri
Cartier-Bresson
Tati at the Cannes
Festival 1958

146 David Seymour *Dinner table, Cagliari, Sardinia* 1954

147 René Burri *Picasso with his children Claude and Paloma, drawing with friends, Le Cannet, France 1957*

148 Robert Capa *Café de Flore, Paris* 1952

149 Dennis Stock *Café de Flore, Paris* 1958

150 Cornell Capa *Bolshoi Ballet School, Moscow* 1958

151 David Seymour *Françoise Sagan* 1956

152 Inge Morath *The Lido, Paris 1958*

153 Burt Glinn *Crazy Horse Saloon, Paris 1956*

154 Henri Cartier-Bresson *Farmer in Normandy* 1960   155 Henri Cartier-Bresson *Farmer in Brittany* 1958

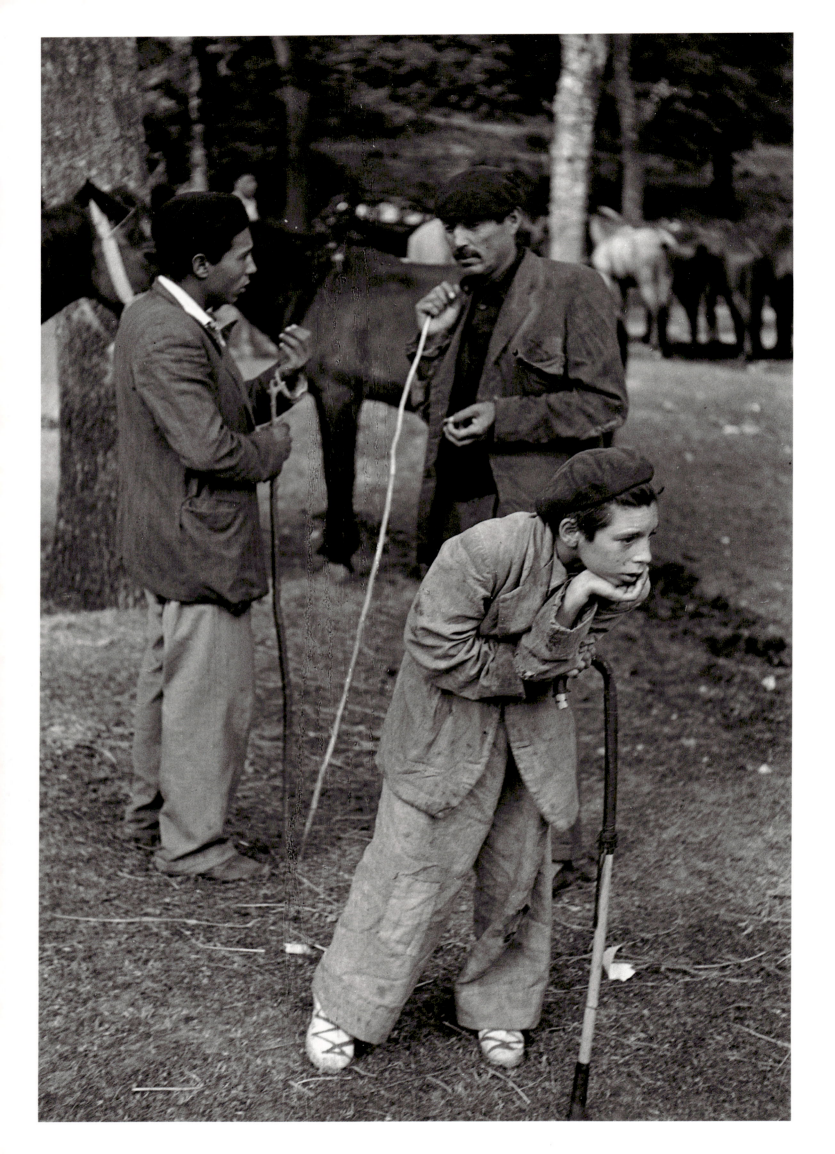

156 Henri Cartier-Bresson *Animal market outside Pamplona, Spain* 1952

157 René Burri *Barn in Czechoslovakia* 1955

158 Philippe Halsman *Jean Cocteau* 1949

159 Marilyn Silverstone *Paris* 1957

160 Marc Riboud *Rue Mouffetard, Paris* 1959

161 Inge Morath *Disabled veterans, Shepherd Market, London* 1954

162 Inge Morath *Enghien-les-Bains, near Paris* 1954

163 Bruce Davidson *Nannies in Hyde Park, London* 1960

164 Burt Glinn *Klosters, Switzerland* 1957

165 Henri Cartier-Bresson *Vélodrome d'hiver, Paris* 1957

166 Erich Lessing *Treasures of the Czars exhibition, Moscow 1958*

LE SOLEIL CONSTITUE LA SOURCE D' ÉNERGIE
POUR L'APPAREILLAGE DU SPOUTNIK

167 Henri Cartier-Bresson *Sputnik display, the USSR Pavilion, Brussels World's Fair 1958*

168 Kryn Taconis
*The Atomium,
Brussels World's Fair 1958*

INDEX OF
PHOTOGRAPHERS